# DASH Diet Slow Cooker Cookbook

15 Minute Set and Forget It DASH Diet Slow Cooker Recipes

Copyright © 2015, Dorothy Kay

All rights Reserved. No part of this publication or the information in it may be quoted from or reproduced in any form by means such as printing, scanning, photocopying or otherwise without prior written permission of the copyright holder.

## Disclaimer and Terms of Use:

Effort has been made to ensure that the information in this book is accurate and complete, however, the author and the publisher do not warrant the accuracy of the information, text and graphics contained within the book due to the rapidly changing nature of science, research, known and unknown facts and internet. The Author and the publisher do not hold any responsibility for errors, omissions or contrary interpretation of the subject matter herein. This book is presented solely for motivational and informational purposes only.

## Table of Contents

Introduction .......................................................................... 5

DASH Diet Slow Cooker Recipes ......................................... 7

    Spinach and Red Pepper Frittata ..................................... 9

    Apple Cinnamon Breakfast Quinoa .............................. 11

    Sweet Potato, Carrot and Walnut Hash ....................... 13

    Blueberry Steel Cut Oats ............................................... 15

    Mixed Vegetable Frittata ............................................... 17

    Cinnamon Steel Cut Oats .............................................. 19

    Easy Spiced Pumpkin Butter ......................................... 21

    Butternut Squash Soup .................................................. 23

    Bean and Turkey Chili .................................................... 25

    Spinach White Bean Soup ............................................. 27

    Curried Sweet Potato Lentil Stew ................................. 29

    Carrot Ginger Soup ........................................................ 31

    Sweet Potato Chickpea Curry ....................................... 33

    Italian Chicken and Capers ........................................... 35

    Beef and Mushroom Burgundy .................................... 37

    Chicken Sausage and Pepper Pasta ............................. 39

    Tomato Herb Chicken Breasts ...................................... 41

    Brown Rice-Stuffed Red Peppers .................................. 43

    Lemon Artichoke Whole-Wheat Pasta ......................... 45

Simple Poached Pears ................................................... 47

Raisin and Walnut-Stuffed Apples ................................ 49

Tropical Bananas Foster ............................................... 51

Cocoa Almonds .............................................................. 53

Cinnamon Brown Rice Pudding .................................... 55

Whole-Wheat Peach Crisp ............................................ 57

Conclusion ......................................................................... 59

# Introduction

There are an endless number of fad diets out there, each one promising different results in an impossibly short time frame. Even if you are not overweight or obese, you have probably tried a few of these diets yourself in the hopes of losing a few pounds or just improving your health. The DASH diet is a popular diet that has been helping countless individuals improve their health and lose weight, all without crash dieting. The DASH diet is not a fad diet – it is a lifestyle choice that is meant to be followed for the long-term and it provides many health benefits including improved eating habits, regular digestion, and (most importantly) stabilized blood pressure levels.

The American Heart Association (AHA) created the DASH diet to provide individuals with a means of lowering their high blood pressure without the use of medication. By improving your eating habits and reducing your sodium intake you can reduce your blood pressure by as much as 6 points in just a few weeks. If you are curious to see what the DASH diet can do for you, then this book is the perfect place to start. Within the pages of this book you will find a collection of 25 delicious DASH diet recipes for the slow cooker. The slow cooker is great because you can just add your ingredients, turn it on and let it cook – what could be easier than that? By using your slow cooker you can cut down on meal prep which will increase your chances of sticking to the diet.

So, if you are ready to give the DASH diet a try, pull out your slow cooker, pick a recipe, and get cooking! You won't be disappointed.

# DASH Diet Slow Cooker Recipes

The DASH diet encourages the consumption of wholesome, nutritious foods to improve your health and eating habits. You do not have to count calories if you don't want to, but you should make an effort to eat less processed food and refined grains in favor of fresh produce, whole grains, and other healthy foods. The staples of the DASH diet are fresh fruits and vegetables, whole grains, nuts and seeds, lean meat and seafood, eggs, and low-fat dairy. The recipes that follow are focused around these ingredients.

## Recipes Included in this Book:

Spinach and Red Pepper Frittata

Apple Cinnamon Breakfast Quinoa

Sweet Potato, Carrot and Walnut Hash

Blueberry Steel Cut Oats

Mixed Vegetable Frittata

Cinnamon Steel Cut Oats

Easy Spiced Pumpkin Butter

Butternut Squash Soup

Bean and Turkey Chili

Spinach White Bean Soup

Curried Sweet Potato Lentil Stew

Carrot Ginger Soup

Sweet Potato Chickpea Curry

Italian Chicken and Capers

Beef and Mushroom Burgundy

Chicken Sausage and Pepper Pasta

Tomato Herb Chicken Breasts

Brown Rice-Stuffed Red Peppers

Lemon Artichoke Whole-Wheat Pasta

Simple Poached Pears

Raisin and Walnut-Stuffed Apples

Tropical Bananas Foster

Cocoa Almonds

Cinnamon Brown Rice Pudding

Whole-Wheat Peach Crisp

## Spinach and Red Pepper Frittata

**Servings**: 6

**Ingredients**:

- 4 large eggs plus 2 whites, beaten well
- ¼ cup fat-free milk
- Salt and pepper to taste
- 2 cups fresh chopped baby spinach
- 1 medium red pepper, cored and chopped
- ½ small yellow onion, chopped

**Instructions**:

1. Grease the insert of your slow cooker with cooking spray.
2. Whisk together the eggs, egg whites, fat-free milk, salt and pepper in a mixing bowl.
3. Pour the mixture into the slow cooker.

4. Add the spinach, onion and red pepper, stirring until evenly spread.
5. Cover and cook on low heat for 1 to 1 ½ hours until the center of the frittata is set.
6. Remove the lid and let cool 5 to 10 minutes before serving.

## Apple Cinnamon Breakfast Quinoa

**Servings**: 6 to 8

**Ingredients**:

- 6 cups water
- 3 cups fat-free milk
- 6 tablespoons pure maple syrup
- 2 tablespoons ground cinnamon
- 1 cup uncooked quinoa, rinsed well
- 1 cup steel-cut oats, uncooked
- 2 medium ripe apples, peeled, cored and diced

**Instructions**:

1. Stir together the water, fat-free milk, maple syrup and cinnamon in the slow cooker.
2. Add the quinoa and oats, stirring well to combine, then fold in the apples.

3. Cover the slow cooker and cook on low heat for 8 to 10 hours until thick and creamy.
4. Spoon into bowls and garnish with fresh apples and chopped walnuts to serve.

## Sweet Potato, Carrot and Walnut Hash

**Servings**: 6 to 8

**Ingredients**:

- 3 medium sweet potatoes, peeled and chopped
- 2 medium carrots, peeled and sliced
- 1 small yellow onion, chopped
- ½ cup vegetable broth
- 1 tablespoon olive oil
- 1 teaspoon minced garlic
- ½ teaspoon dried thyme
- Salt and pepper to taste
- 1/3 cup chopped walnuts

**Instructions**:

1. Combine the sweet potatoes, carrots and onions in the slow cooker.

2. Stir in the vegetable broth, olive oil, garlic, thyme, salt and pepper.
3. Cover the slow cooker and cook on low heat for 3 to 4 hours until the sweet potatoes are tender.
4. Stir the walnuts in during the last 20 minutes of cooking. Serve hot.

## Blueberry Steel Cut Oats

**Servings**: 6 to 8

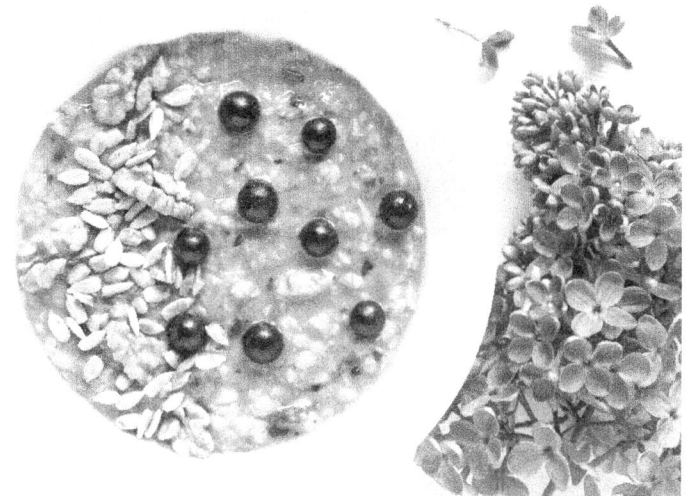

**Ingredients**:

- 4 cups water
- 3 cups fat-free milk
- ¼ cup raw honey
- 2 cups steel-cut oats
- ¼ cup ground flaxseed
- Pinch salt
- 1 cup fresh blueberries
- 1 teaspoon vanilla extract

**Instructions**:

1. Whisk together the water, fat-free milk and honey in the slow cooker.
2. Stir in the oats, ground flaxseed and salt.

3. Cover the slow cooker and cook on low heat for 6 to 7 hours or on high heat for 2 to 2 ½ hours until thick and creamy.
4. Mash the blueberries gently with a fork then stir them into the slow cooker along with the vanilla extract.
5. Spoon into bowls and garnish with fresh blueberries to serve.

## Mixed Vegetable Frittata

**Servings**: 6

**Ingredients**:

- 4 large eggs plus 2 whites, beaten well
- ¼ cup fat-free milk
- Salt and pepper to taste
- 1 (14-ounce) can diced tomatoes, drained
- 1 medium red pepper, cored and chopped
- 1 medium green pepper, cored and chopped
- ½ small yellow onion, chopped
- 1 teaspoon minced garlic

**Instructions**:

1. Grease the insert of your slow cooker with cooking spray.
2. Whisk together the eggs, egg whites, fat-free milk, salt and pepper in a mixing bowl.

3. Pour the mixture into the slow cooker.
4. Add the tomatoes, peppers, onion and garlic, stirring until evenly spread.
5. Cover and cook on low heat for 1 to 1 ½ hours until the center of the frittata is set.
6. Remove the lid and let cool 5 to 10 minutes before serving.

## Cinnamon Steel Cut Oats

**Servings**: 6 to 8

**Ingredients**:

- 8 cups cold water
- 1 ½ cups fat-free milk
- 1 teaspoon vanilla extract
- 1 teaspoon ground cinnamon
- Pinch salt
- 2 cups steel-cut oats
- ¼ cup raw honey

**Instructions**:

1. Stir together the water, milk vanilla extract, cinnamon and salt in the slow cooker.
2. Add the oats and honey, stirring until thoroughly combined.

3. Cover the slow cooker and cook on low heat for 7 to 8 hours until thick and creamy.
4. Spoon the oats into bowls and top with fresh fruit and chopped nuts to serve.

## Easy Spiced Pumpkin Butter

**Servings**: Makes 2 cups

**Ingredients**:

- 4 (15-ounce) cans pumpkin puree
- 1 ½ cups pure maple syrup
- 1 ½ teaspoon vanilla extract
- 1 tablespoon ground cinnamon
- 1 teaspoon ground ginger
- ½ teaspoon ground nutmeg

**Instructions**:

1. Lightly grease the insert of the slow cooker with cooking spray.
2. Combine the pumpkin, maple syrup and vanilla in the slow cooker.
3. Cover and cook on high heat for 3 to 4 hours or on low for 7 to 8 hours.

4. Stir in the cinnamon, ginger and nutmeg during the last hour of cooking.

## Butternut Squash Soup

**Servings**: 6 to 8

**Ingredients**:

- 1 large butternut squash (about 2 lbs.)
- 1 small yellow onion, chopped
- 1 large ripe apple, cored, peeled and chopped
- 1 medium carrot, peeled and chopped
- 1 teaspoon minced garlic
- 2 cups chicken broth or vegetable broth
- ½ teaspoon dried thyme
- Salt and pepper to taste

**Instructions**:

1. Cut the butternut squash in half and discard the seeds.
2. Peel the squash and cut the flesh into chunks then add them to the slow cooker.

3. Add the onion, apples, carrot and garlic.
4. Stir together the remaining ingredients and pour into the slow cooker.
5. Cover and cook on low heat for 6 to 8 hours or on high for 3 to 4 hours.
6. Turn off the heat and puree the soup using an immersion blender until smooth. Serve hot.

## Bean and Turkey Chili

**Servings**: 6 to 8

**Ingredients**:

- 1 tablespoon olive oil
- 2 lbs. lean ground turkey breast
- 1 large yellow onion, chopped
- 2 teaspoons chili powder
- 1 teaspoon minced garlic
- ½ teaspoon ground cumin
- Salt and pepper to taste
- 2 (14.5-ounce) cans diced tomatoes, drained
- 1 (15-ounce) can red kidney beans, rinsed and drained
- 1 (15-ounce) can pinto beans, rinsed and drained
- 1 cup water

**Instructions**:

1. Heat the oil in a large skillet over medium heat.
2. Add the turkey, onion, chili powder, cumin, and garlic then season with salt and pepper to taste.
3. Cook for 4 to 5 minutes until the turkey is browned then spoon the mixture into the slow cooker.
4. Stir in the tomatoes, beans, and water.
5. Cover the slow cooker and cook for 8 to 10 hours on low until the beans are tender.

## Spinach White Bean Soup

**Servings**: 6 to 8

**Ingredients**:

- 1 large yellow onion, chopped
- ½ cup uncooked brown rice
- 1 teaspoon minced garlic
- 6 cups low-sodium vegetable broth
- 1 (15-ounce) can white cannellini beans, rinsed and drained
- ¼ cup fresh chopped basil
- Salt and pepper to taste
- 6 to 8 cups fresh chopped baby spinach

**Instructions**:

1. Combine the onions, rice and garlic in the slow cooker.
2. Stir in the vegetable broth, beans, and basil.

3. Season with salt and pepper to taste then cover the slow cooker.
4. Cook on low heat for 6 to 8 hours then stir in the spinach.
5. Let rest for 5 to 10 minutes until wilted then spoon the soup into bowls and serve hot.

## Curried Sweet Potato Lentil Stew

**Servings**: 6 to 8

**Ingredients**:

- 2 large sweet potatoes, peeled and chopped
- 2 large carrots, peeled and diced
- 1 large yellow onion, chopped
- 1 cup uncooked red lentils, rinsed well
- 2 ½ cups low-sodium vegetable broth
- 1 teaspoon minced garlic
- ½ teaspoon fresh grated ginger
- 1 tablespoon curry powder
- Salt and pepper to taste

**Instructions**:

1. Stir together the sweet potatoes, carrots, and onions in the slow cooker.

2. Add the lentils and vegetable broth then stir in the remaining ingredients.
3. Cover and cook on low heat for 5 to 6 hours until the lentils are very tender.
4. Spoon the stew into bowls and serve garnished with fresh chopped kale.

## Carrot Ginger Soup

**Servings**: 6 to 8

**Ingredients**:

- 10 large carrots, peeled and chopped
- 1 large yellow onion, chopped
- 1 tablespoon fresh grated ginger
- 6 cups low-sodium chicken broth
- ½ cup canned coconut milk
- ½ teaspoon curry powder
- Salt and pepper to taste

**Instructions**:

1. Combine the carrots, onion, and ginger in the slow cooker.
2. Stir in the broth, coconut milk and curry powder.
3. Cover the slow cooker and cook on low heat for 7 to 8 hours until the vegetables are tender.

4. Season with salt and pepper to taste then puree using an immersion blender. Serve hot.

## Sweet Potato Chickpea Curry

**Servings**: 6 to 8

**Ingredients**:

- 2 large sweet potatoes, peeled and chopped
- 1 large yellow onion, chopped
- 1 tablespoon fresh grated ginger
- 1 teaspoon minced garlic
- 2 (15-ounce) cans chickpeas, rinsed and drained
- 2 (14-ounce) cans low-sodium chicken broth
- 1 (14-ounce) can diced tomatoes, drained
- 1 cup chopped carrots
- 1 tablespoon curry powder
- 1 teaspoon ground turmeric
- Salt and pepper to taste

**Instructions**:

1. Combine the sweet potatoes, onion, ginger and garlic in the slow cooker.
2. Stir in the chickpeas, vegetable broth, carrots, tomatoes and seasonings.
3. Cover and cook on low heat for 8 to 10 hours or on high for 3 to 4 hours until the vegetables are very tender.
4. Season with salt and pepper to taste then serve hot.

## Italian Chicken and Capers

**Servings**: 6

**Ingredients**:

- ½ cup balsamic vinegar
- 1 ½ tablespoons Dijon mustard
- 1 teaspoon fresh lemon juice
- 1 clove minced garlic
- 6 boneless skinless chicken breasts
- Salt and pepper to taste
- ¼ cup capers, drained

**Instructions**:

1. Lightly grease the insert of your slow cooker with cooking spray.
2. Whisk together the vinegar, mustard, lemon juice, and garlic in a bowl.

3. Season the chicken breasts with salt and pepper to taste then place them in the slow cooker.
4. Pour in the sauce and capers then cover the slow cooker.
5. Cook on low heat for 5 to 6 hours until the chicken is cooked through. Serve hot.

## Beef and Mushroom Burgundy

**Servings**: 6 to 8

**Ingredients**:

- 2 lbs. beef stew meat, cut into chunks
- Salt and pepper to taste
- ¼ cup whole-wheat flour
- 2 cups sliced mushrooms
- 1 large yellow onion, chopped
- 1 (14-ounce) can diced tomatoes in juice
- ½ cup beef broth
- 1 teaspoon dried oregano
- ½ teaspoon dried thyme

**Instructions**:

1. Lightly grease the insert of your slow cooker with cooking spray.

2. Season the beef with salt and pepper to taste then toss with flour.
3. Spread the beef in the slow cooker then add the mushrooms and onions.
4. Pour in the diced tomatoes and beef broth then sprinkle in the oregano and thyme.
5. Cover the slow cooker and cook on low heat for 7 to 8 hours until the beef is tender.

## Chicken Sausage and Pepper Pasta

**Servings**: 6 to 8

**Ingredients**:

- 2 ½ lbs. Italian chicken sausage links, sliced
- 3 large red peppers, cored and sliced
- 1 large yellow onion, sliced
- 2 (14-ounce) cans tomato sauce
- 12 to 16 ounces whole-wheat pasta

**Instructions**:

1. Lightly grease the insert of your slow cooker with cooking spray.
2. Toss together the chicken sausage, red peppers and onion in the slow cooker.
3. Pour in the tomato sauce then cover the slow cooker.
4. Cook on low heat for 6 to 8 hours.

5. Meanwhile, bring a large pot of salted water to boil.
6. Add the pasta and cook to al dente – about 8 to 10 minutes – then drain.
7. Stir the drained pasta into the slow cooker and serve hot.

## Tomato Herb Chicken Breasts

**Servings**: 6 to 8

**Ingredients**:

- 6 boneless skinless chicken breasts
- Salt and pepper to taste
- 2 cups bottled Alfredo sauce
- 1 (14-ounce) can tomato sauce
- 1 (14-ounce) can diced tomatoes, drained
- 3 cloves minced garlic
- 2 tablespoons fresh chopped basil
- 2 tablespoons fresh chopped parsley
- 1 teaspoon fresh chopped oregano

**Instructions**:

1. Lightly grease the insert of your slow cooker with cooking spray.

2. Season the chicken breasts with salt and pepper then place them in the slow cooker.
3. Whisk together the remaining ingredients and pour over the chicken.
4. Cover and cook on low heat for 6 to 7 hours until the chicken is cooked through. Serve hot.

## Brown Rice-Stuffed Red Peppers

**Servings**: 6

**Ingredients**:

- 6 medium red bell peppers
- 1 ½ lbs. lean ground turkey breast
- 2 cups steamed brown rice
- 1 small yellow onion, chopped
- ½ cup fresh diced tomatoes
- 1 teaspoon minced garlic
- Salt and pepper to taste

**Instructions**:

1. Lightly grease the insert of your slow cooker with cooking spray.
2. Slice the tops off the red peppers and take out the core and seeds.

3. Stir together the turkey, tomatoes, onion, garlic and rice in a bowl.
4. Place the peppers upright in the slow cooker and spoon the rice mixture into them.
5. Season with salt and pepper to taste then cover the slow cooker.
6. Cook on low heat for 6 hours until tender.

## Lemon Artichoke Whole-Wheat Pasta

**Servings**: 6 to 8

**Ingredients**:

- 2 (14-ounce) cans artichoke hearts, drained and chopped
- 1 cup fresh sliced mushrooms
- 1 medium yellow onion, chopped
- 1 teaspoon minced garlic
- ½ cup half-and-half
- 2 tablespoons fresh lemon juice
- 12 to 16 ounces whole-wheat pasta

**Instructions**:

1. Lightly grease the insert of your slow cooker with cooking spray.
2. Toss together the artichoke hearts, mushrooms, onions and garlic in the slow cooker.

3. Cover and cook on low heat for 6 to 8 hours.
4. Pour in the half-and-half and lemon juice then cover the slow cooker and let stand.
5. Meanwhile, bring a large pot of salted water to boil.
6. Add the pasta and cook to al dente – about 8 to 10 minutes – then drain.
7. Stir the drained pasta into the slow cooker and serve hot.

## Simple Poached Pears

**Servings**: 6

**Ingredients**:

- 6 large ripe pears, peeled
- 2 cups unsweetened apple juice
- ¼ cup raw honey
- ¼ cup fresh squeezed orange juice
- 1 teaspoon vanilla extract
- ½ teaspoon ground cinnamon
- Pinch ground nutmeg
- Pinch ground cloves

**Instructions**:

1. Use a small knife to remove the core from the pears at the bottom.
2. Place the pears upright in the slow cooker.

3. Whisk together the remaining ingredients and pour into the slow cooker.
4. Cover and cook for 3 hours on high heat until the pears are soft. Serve hot.

## Raisin and Walnut-Stuffed Apples

**Servings**: 6

**Ingredients**:

- 6 medium ripe apples
- 1 cup unsweetened apple juice
- ½ cup seedless raisins
- ¼ cup chopped walnuts
- 2 tablespoons brown sugar
- 1 teaspoon ground cinnamon
- ¼ teaspoon ground nutmeg

**Instructions**:

1. Slice the tops off the apples and carefully scoop out the cores from the top.
2. Place the apples upright in the slow cooker and pour in the apple juice around them.

3. Combine the remaining ingredients in a bowl then spoon into the apples.
4. Cover the slow cooker and cook on low heat for 2 to 3 hours until the apples are tender.

## Tropical Bananas Foster

**Servings**: 6 to 8

**Ingredients**:

- ½ cup fat-free milk
- ½ cup light brown sugar, packed
- 3 tablespoons margarine
- 5 large ripe bananas, peeled and sliced
- 1 cup fresh chopped pineapple
- ½ teaspoon ground cinnamon

**Instructions**:

1. Grease the insert of your slow cooker with cooking spray.
2. Combine the milk, light brown sugar and margarine in the slow cooker.
3. Cover and cook on low heat for 1 hour then stir smooth.

4. Toss in the bananas and pineapple then sprinkle with cinnamon.
5. Cover and cook on low heat for 15 minutes until tender.
6. Spoon into bowls and serve drizzled with coconut milk.

## Cocoa Almonds

**Servings**: makes 3 cups

**Ingredients**:

- 3 cups raw almonds
- 3 tablespoons margarine
- 2 to 3 tablespoons unsweetened cocoa powder
- 1 ½ teaspoons vanilla extract
- Up to ¼ teaspoon powdered stevia

**Instructions**:

1. Toss together the almonds, margarine, cocoa powder, vanilla and stevia in the slow cooker.
2. Cover and cook on high heat for 1 hour then stir and cook for another 30 minutes.
3. Spread the nuts out on baking sheets lined with parchment to cool then store in airtight containers.

## Cinnamon Brown Rice Pudding

**Servings**: 6 to 8

**Ingredients**:

- 1 cup long-grain brown rice
- 1/3 cup light brown sugar, packed
- 1 ½ teaspoon ground cinnamon
- 3 ¼ cups nonfat milk
- 1 ½ teaspoon vanilla extract

**Instructions**:

1. Combine the rice, brown sugar and cinnamon in the slow cooker.
2. Stir in the milk then cover the slow cooker.
3. Cook on low heat for 3 to 4 hours until the rice is tender and thick.
4. Stir in the vanilla extract then turn off the heat.
5. Spoon into bowls and serve hot.

## Whole-Wheat Peach Crisp

**Servings**: 6 to 8

**Ingredients**:

- 4 cups fresh sliced peaches
- 2 tablespoons honey
- 1 tablespoon fresh lemon juice
- 1 ½ teaspoons vanilla extract
- 2/3 cups whole-wheat pastry flour
- 2/3 cups old-fashioned oats
- ½ cup light brown sugar, packed
- 2 teaspoons ground cinnamon
- ½ teaspoon ground nutmeg
- Pinch salt

**Instructions**:

1. Grease the insert of your slow cooker with cooking spray.

2. Toss the peaches with the honey, lemon juice and vanilla then spread in the slow cooker.
3. In a bowl, combine the flour, oats, brown sugar, cinnamon, nutmeg and salt.
4. Cut in the margarine until it forms a crumbled mixture.
5. Spread the crumbled mixture over the peaches and cover the slow cooker.
6. Cook on high heat for 2 hours until hot and bubbling.

# Conclusion

If you struggle with high blood pressure, take a moment to think before you call up your doctor and ask for a prescription. The DASH diet is backed by years of research and it has been proven effective as a means of naturally reducing blood pressure. If you want to improve your health and reduce your blood pressure, give the DASH diet a try by starting with some of the recipes in this book. Because these recipes can be prepared in your slow cooker they are incredibly easy – most take no more than 10 minutes of prep time. So, if you are ready to try the DASH Diet for yourself, pick a recipe and start cooking!

Made in the USA
Coppell, TX
15 January 2022